Remarkable Islander

RIPPING YARNS

By Ian Williams

Published By
COACH HOUSE PUBLICATIONS
LIMITED

Publishers Details

Copyright ©
COACH HOUSE PUBLICATIONS LIMITED 2006

All rights reserved. No part of this work covered by the copyrights hereon may be reproduced or used in any form or by any means - graphic, electronic or mechanical, including photocopying, recording, taping of information on storage and retrieval systems - without the prior written permission of the publisher.

ISBN: 1-899-392-475

October 2006

Printed in the UK

Published By
COACH HOUSE PUBLICATIONS LIMITED
ISLE OF WIGHT, ENGLAND

THE COACH HOUSE, SCHOOL GREEN ROAD,
FRESHWATER, ISLE OF WIGHT, PO40 9BB.
TEL: +44 (0) 1983 755655

Further copies of this book and other Island books can be obtained from the publishers by contacting us at the address above or via our online ordering service at:
www.coachhouseonline.co.uk

Book Design By DAVID BOWLES

Remarkable Islanders

Contents

Introduction
PAGES 01 to 02

'Galloper' Jack Seely
PAGES 03 to 08

The Man The Turks Couldn't Kill
PAGES 09 to 11

Outlaw Turned Hero
PAGES 12 to 16

Arctic Apostle
PAGES 17 to 23

Admiral 'Snip'
PAGES 24 to 27

The Woeful Woodvilles
PAGES 28 to 35

Prisoner Of Conscience
⋈ PAGES 36 to 42 ⋈

The Dragon Hunter
⋈ PAGES 43 to 46 ⋈

The Queen Of Chantilly
⋈ PAGES 47 to 51 ⋈

England's Leonardo
⋈ PAGES 52 to 55 ⋈

The Moralising Maid
⋈ PAGES 56 to 59 ⋈

The Natural Historian
⋈ PAGES 60 to 62 ⋈

Public Health Pioneer
⋈ PAGES 63 to 66 ⋈

The Hurricane Pilot
⋈ PAGES 67 to 71 ⋈

Unpredictable Uffa
⋈ PAGES 72 to 76 ⋈

The Swashbuckling Captain
⋈ PAGES 77 to 81 ⋈

Remarkable Islanders

Ripping Yarns

By Ian Williams

Remarkable Islanders

INTRODUCTION

Remarkable Islanders needs an explanation. Just who is an islander is a subject for passionate pub debate. Hardliners would argue that if you can't trace your ancestry back several generations, if not centuries, you are not a true islander; new arrivals, on the other hand, claim residence alone is sufficient for the label islander to apply.

Being born on the island confers a permanent status, an indelible place of origin that is indisputable. The born islander may not remain an islander for long, but be whisked away by parents to 'the mainland' before he or she is sensible of their origins or is capable of making a contribution to the community. But an islander they remain. Death confers no such status; 'overners' who die on the island remain 'overners.'

Living on an island makes us all islanders, no matter from where we came or where we end up. Residence, however long or short the stay, allows those of us not born here to share the label 'islander' though to some, 'overners' will always be 'overners.' Most of these remarkable islanders were born here; the others, while resident here, made significant contributions to island life.

Why remarkable? 'Famous' was inadequate; some, like Sophie Dawes were more notorious than famous and though many of these islanders acquired fame in their day, their star has waned. 'Forgotten Heroes' was suggested but

Jack Seely has not been forgotten and hero is too narrow a definition and is associated with acts of bravery in war. It is not Sid Porter's heroics which make these pages but his miraculous good luck! 'Outstanding islanders' is nearer the mark but is more judgmental whereas 'remarkable' is neutral. For someone to be remarkable they must be striking, out of the ordinary, whether for good or bad. I hope you will agree these are *Remarkable Islanders*.

Remarkable Islanders

'Galloper' Jack Seely

Jack Seely on Maharajah, 1899

Jack Seely was a man who lived dangerously and his charmed life was a series of adventures and escapes straight out of *Boy's Own* comic. Lord Birkenhead wrote: "A contemporary or future Dumas might consider taking Jack Seely as the principal hero of a book of adventure no whit less sensational than *The Three Muskateers*. He would find him as gay, as gallant, as debonair, and, often, as rash as D'Artagnan." He had at least fourteen near death experiences involving each of the elements – earth, air, fire and water.

Jack was born in 1868, the younger son of Charles 'Pig' Seely MP who made his fortune selling pig iron to the Royal Navy. Jack was brought up on the Isle of Wight on the family estate at Brook and as a boy of nine survived a cliff fall of seventy feet. It was a miraculous escape and proved to young Jack "that fear was foolish, and that no case, however desperate, is ever hopeless." It also had the great merit of earning him a term's holiday from school.

Having survived a potentially fatal fall he nearly drowned in a swimming baths, an experience he brought on himself. In a foolish contest of "Diving for Eggs" Jack took one stroke underwater too many, blacked out and had to be resuscitated.

At the age of 20 Jack and his friend Tom Conolly holidayed at Davos in the Swiss Alps. Jack took Catherine, Tom's twelve year old sister, on a 'promenade au cheval' up to a mountain pass on borrowed horses. Jack's horse was a thoroughbred, 16 hands high, and of a wild disposition. After a stop at an inn Jack's horse broke free then bolted at breakneck speed with no bridle to control him. The horse came down with a crash and Jack found himself face in the dirt with his legs dangling over a chasm. He was brought home to England with cushions and ice boxes round his head and was laid up for months with "congestion of the brain."

On 19 October 1891, Jack helped rescue the crew of a French brig, the *Henri Leontine*, that came ashore on Brook Ledge. Though close to shore the crew were separated by the pounding surf from the safety of land. Three men and a boy left the brig on a makeshift breeches buoy; Jack and a coastguardman entered the raging surf to meet them half way and help them ashore. For his "outstanding gallantry" the French government awarded Jack their top civilian medal, 'La Medaille d'Or d'Honneur'.

During that rescue some floating wreckage drove a rib into his lung and doctors advised a long sea voyage. So Jack sailed with Tom Conolly to New Zealand via the Cape but not content to enjoy the journey as passengers, they accepted a bet that they would act as able seamen. The captain agreed and they shared all the hardships of the crew from the Cape to New Zealand. Once there they trekked across the country on horseback, Jack surviving another near drowning while trying to ford a river in spate.

Back at Brook in January 1894 Jack responded to the maroon calling out the lifeboat to help the steamer *Ossian* which had gone aground. One of the lifeboat crew was ill and Jack was put in to row stroke on the port side. They rescued seven crew and Ben Jacobs, the coxswain, proposed Jack as a permanent member of the crew. As a result of his soaking Jack contracted pneumonia and pleurisy, coming close to death. He claims he heard a nurse say, "I'm afraid he has gone, a nice sort of boy too." Told he must give up all hope of an active life, he was sent on a boat down the Nile to recuperate; miraculously, within three weeks, Jack was back to full fitness.

Acts of physical courage, some would say foolhardiness, recur throughout his life. In 1900, while serving in the Boer War as a Captain in the Hampshire

Yeomanry, he refused to leave two troops of his men to fight a desperate rearguard action without him, contrary to orders. Though court-martialled Seely received only a reprimand and praise for the "efficient manner" of his defence. He was later awarded the DSO.

Later in the war, after riding up to a kraal for observations Seely was confronted by three Boers. One of them raised his rifle and aimed at him from 12 yards. Jack calmly awaited his end when an extraordinary thing happened. "The man lowered his rifle, looked me straight in the eyes, turned round and walked away." Jack's luck held but for how much longer could he evade death?

Jack Seely was elected Conservative MP for the Isle of Wight while still in South Africa. After switching his allegiance to the Liberals he and Winston Churchill became their party's rising stars. By 1912 they were Cabinet colleagues, Seely being appointed as Secretary of State for War. In August 1914, now an ex-Minister as a result of the Curragh crisis, Jack Seely went to Farnborough for a demonstration flight in an aeroplane. Well into the flight Jack, who was in the front seat, was hit by a splash of escaping petrol. The pilot, a man named Busk, switched off the engine instantly and they made a miraculous crash landing from which they both walked away uninjured. Busk remarked later that he couldn't understand why they didn't both get "frizzed up." It seems that Jack's guardian angel was working overtime!

At the outbreak of war in 1914 Jack was appointed as Special Service Officer to the Expeditionary Force reporting direct to Sir John French. But Jack wanted to command and take his chance in the line and in 1915 Lord Kitchener appointed him to command a Canadian Cavalry Brigade. Seely's grandson, Brough Scott wrote, "to the outsider they looked a displaced, half-trained, makeshift bunch of ranchers, clerks, cowboys, ex-pats, mounties and Red Indians." But they and Seely were "made for each other."

Together they saw action at the Western Front at Festubert, the Somme, Passchendaele and Cambrai. During the great German offensive of 1918 Seely's brigade stormed the Moreuil Ridge, an action which helped secure Amiens. Jack Seely admits to the most astonishing luck. In his biography, aptly titled *Adventure*, he writes "over and over again on the Western Front I have found myself alone unharmed when every one of those around me has been killed or wounded . . . such experiences have left me with an abiding sense of gratitude to the unseen hand which has protected me so often."

But Jack didn't come through the war unscathed. During an action to capture Fisher's Crater, galloping on his pony *Akbar*, a shell exploded nearby felling the pony with Jack trapped beneath. Broken bones and internal bleeding earned him a 'blighty' and he recovered at Brook. But he could not abandon his brigade and engineered a warrant passing him as fit for service abroad when he could barely walk.

As if this were not enough Jack Seely was gassed in 1918 swallowing all three kinds – chlorine, mustard and some of the deadly phosgene. In hospital near Etaples he was told he was lucky to be alive. Jack's horse *Warrior* shared his luck for it survived the whole war and went on to win the Isle of Wight Point-to-Point on the anniversary of the Battle of Moreuil in 1922!

'Galloper' Jack Seely was many things: pampered son of a rich industrialist, decorated war hero, politician and senior Cabinet Minister, gallant lifeboatman. Jack was a colourful character, one of a dying breed for whom

Nation and Empire, and the comradeship of fellow soldiers, meant everything. But his life's record was marred by a naïve flirtation with fascism; great patriot though he was, he met and fell under the spell of both Hitler and Mussolini and he became the mouthpiece for their achievements. Despite the warnings of his friends he became an unrepentant apologist for Nazi Germany and appeasement, though when war inevitably came he was quick to enter the fray and offer his services to his country. On 7 November 1947 Seely's gas-wrecked chest finally gave up.

Remarkable Islanders

❦ THE MAN THE TURKS COULDN'T KILL ❦

SIDNEY PORTER

When Rifleman Sid Porter left Liverpool at 1.00pm on 30 July 1915 aboard the *Aquitania* he could have had no idea what was in store for him in less than two weeks time. Porter was a signaller with the 1st/8th Battalion Hampshire Regiment (Princess Beatrice's Isle of Wight Rifles) bound for Gallipoli and a disastrous campaign against the Turks.

The Isle of Wight Rifles landed at Suvla Bay on 10 August and were kept in reserve for two days. The landings were made without much opposition but the Turks were quietly bringing up reinforcements to the ridge of hills overlooking the Bay. At the foot of these hills were two villages known as Little Anafarta and Big Anafarta; between them and the beach lay the Anafarta

Plain, part of which was covered by a dried up salt lake. The plain, partly cultivated, was covered with patches of scrub and dotted with small trees. It was across this plain that the Isle of Wight Rifles advanced at 4.45pm on the afternoon of 12 August. As Bugle Major Reg Peachey sounded the advance, the sun glinted on his silver bugle and he was hit by a Turkish sniper. He was one of the first to fall and it was a taste of worse to come.

A premonition of disaster came to Captain Clayton Ratsey. He'd missed the morning's briefing and when told the objective said, "My God we'll all be killed." He and his brother, Captain Donald Ratsey, were to perish that day along with three Urry brothers. They were among the eight officers and over three hundred other ranks killed or missing on that first day. But rifleman Sid Porter was destined not to die.

As Porter advanced the troops came under heavy fire from machine guns, snipers and shrapnel from exploding shells. A piece of flying shrapnel entered Sid's thigh and he lay in the dirt unable to move. The advance halted and the troops began to straggle back. Sid called for help but the Turks were hot on their heels and he was left to his fate.

With Turks all around him he pretended to be dead but one soldier wasn't fooled and shot him through the neck. Luckily, it missed his spine and artery. When he came to a Turk saw he was still alive and bayoneted him several times and left him for dead. But he came round again and was bayoneted once more.

When Porter regained consciousness it was to see the Turks digging his grave. One of the digging party, seeing him still alive, beat him unconscious with a shovel. But he refused to die and perhaps the Turks too recognised he was destined to survive for when he came round again he was offered a water bottle instead of the point of a bayonet!

Sid Porter was roped up and taken into captivity, spending the rest of the war in prisoner of war camps. His wounds slowly healed but the wound to his thigh required an operation which was performed without anaesthetic, just four burly prisoners to hold him down. He recovered and became the camp barber. When he finally made it home to the Isle of Wight, Sid set up a barber shop in Newport with his brother and continued in business for fifty years.

Of his treatment by the Turks Sid was very forgiving. "It was in the heat of battle," he said. "They did it in the excitement of the moment. "The only time Sid thought he was going to die was suffering from sunstroke at Smyrna on the way home!

SUPPLY WAGON, SUVLA BAY

TROOPS ADVANCING ACROSS THE ANAFARTA PLAIN

Remarkable Islanders

⚔ Outlaw Turned Hero ⚔

James Buckett, proud coxswain

Convicted smuggler James Buckett more than repaid his debt to society by helping to save the lives of shipwrecked mariners off the treacherous coast of the 'Back of the Wight.' His son recalls: "He saved 280 lives altogether ... and from being an outlaw became a public favourite on whose birthday the church bells used to ring."

Born in the year of Trafalgar, on 14 April 1805, James' life was tied to the sea. He was a fisherman and sailor and didn't finally retire from fishing till he was eighty-two. He was coxswain of the Brighstone lifeboat for nearly twenty years from August 1860, when the first lifeboat was placed on station at Grange Chine, till February 1879 when he decided to retire at the age of seventy-four after a successful rescue of the fourteen crew of the barque *Alpheus Marshall*.

Before he was twenty James was engaged in smuggling tubs of brandy across the channel in a 20-foot wherry, *The Bet*, hiding his tubs at William 'Bung' Russell's house at Moortown, Brighstone. Most of the inhabitants of the 'Back of the Wight' supported the smugglers for they earnt good money in the shore gangs and benefited from cheap drink. But it wasn't without risk. Taking an open boat across to France could be perilous if a storm broke. Once, James was delayed in France by bad weather so long that locals started a collection for his wife and children, convinced he was lost.

There was always the chance of being caught by one of the revenue cutters that prowled up and down the Channel, especially in a small boat heavily laden. James had a few close shaves, ashore and afloat. On one occasion James and his confederates crossed to France by the Southampton packet, purchased their tubs, then hired a French lugger to bring them back. They were caught by a revenue cutter and eventually tried at Winchester but were acquitted through lack of evidence.

James' wife begged him to give it up and James agreed but only after another run. But his luck ran out. He was caught, convicted at Winchester and pressed into the navy for five years. It was what his wife feared for though life in the navy was rough, with harsh discipline and bad food, she would be left to look after herself and her family alone and that could mean the workhouse.

On the 8 August 1832 James joined the crew of *HMS Gannet*. After a year he was promoted to Ordinary Seaman and later to Able Seaman, having been transferred to *HMS Forte*. In all he served four years and eight months with four months remission for good conduct. On his discharge, in May 1837 aged 32, he was rated as Captain of the Foretop. He returned home a reformed character.

There was no doubting that James Bucket was an experienced seaman of great skill and courage and was the natural choice to be coxswain of the Brighstone lifeboat, at the age of fifty-five. The *Rescue* was donated by the Royal Victoria Yacht Club and it is ironic that her first call was to come to the aid of the barque *Cedarine*, a convict ship returning from Bermuda with 191 convicts aboard who had served their time and were returning home. She ran aground on 2 April 1862 and the *Rescue* made eight trips taking off 134 people including all the women and children. The rest were helped ashore by the Coastguards in a beach rescue.

The launching of a lifeboat was a spectacular affair involving up to sixty people and ten or more horses. The boat was thirty foot long, unsinkable and self-righting, and with a thick, heavy hull that made it difficult to launch, row and sail. The team of horses would haul the boat to the water's edge, turn her round to face the waves, then back the carriage far enough into the sea so that when the boat was launched she would have enough water to float. The ten oarsmen and shore party of over thirty 'launchers' would then await the signal from the coxswain.

It was vital that the coxswain had the trust and confidence of the crew and helpers because his judgment and experience were critical to a successful launch. The coxswain had to choose just the right moment, launching into a large, long wave big enough to float the boat but not so big as to capsize her. Too early or too late and they would all be in the water and it would take an hour before they were ready to try again.

On the order from the coxswain, the helpers had to react instantly and haul on the lines with all their strength to shoot the boat off the carriage and into the surf. For their part, the oarsmen had to ensure they pulled together the moment they were afloat and make a second stroke before the next wave struck. Add to this a black night, the howling wind and lashing rain, the roar of the surf, jangling of harness and shouts of helpers, the rumble as the boat slides seawards, the oarsmen drenched and cold and something of the atmosphere of a launch can be conjured.

It was just such a night, on 3 February 1873, with strong east-south-easterly winds and rain, snow and sleet that the 640-ton steamer *Woodham*, adrift with a broken propeller shaft, grounded at Chilton Chine at two in the morning. The *Rescue* arrived and took off the twenty crew in two trips but the captain and mate remained aboard. With the boat rehoused and the crew making for home the distress signal went up again.

The lifeboat was relaunched "under very dangerous circumstances and in terribly severe weather" and took off the two men. The minute book records the crew were "severely tried and exhausted" that night and James Buckett was awarded the RNLI Silver Medal for his gallantry.

LIFEBOAT RESCUE, BACK OF THE WIGHT

THE COTTAGE AT BRIGHSTONE WHERE JAMES BUCKETT HID HIS TUBS

Remarkable Islanders

⚜ Arctic Apostle ⚜

Edgar Greenshield

In the early years of the twentieth century, the last great wildernesses on earth that remained largely unknown were the Arctic and the Antarctic. It was the great age of polar exploration, of Nansen and Shackleton, Scott and Amundsen. There was huge public interest in the exploits of these men and the Isle of Wight has its own forgotten hero of the Arctic – Edgar William Tyler Greenshield. Between 1901-1913 he made five extensive journeys to the harsh world of the Arctic, working as a missionary among the eskimos of Baffin Island. He rescued the crew of a Dutch schooner and became something of a minor celebrity and a popular speaker.

Edgar Greenshield was born on 22 November 1877, son of a Newport draper. He was educated at the Portland House Academy which he later described as producing "empire-builders, thanks largely to the priceless qualities and principles instilled in us". But the centre of family life was unquestionably their church, St John's, Newport. The Rev Henry Lewis, Vicar from 1892 to 1896, had spent seven years as a missionary in India and was a compelling speaker. It was after hearing a sermon from Lewis that Greenshield determined to devote his life to mission work.

At 20 he joined the Church Missionary Society and attended their Theological College at Islington on a three year course. As well as traditional subjects, students were taught medical and technical skills (technical classes included printing, tin-smithing, blacksmithing, cobbling and carpentry) so that, once in the field, they could deal with any emergency. In 1901, as he embarked on his final year, Greenshield's childhood dream to visit the Arctic came true. The College received a call from the Rev Peck for immediate assistance amongst the eskimos of Baffin Island. Greenshield jumped at the chance and set sail from Peterhead in Scotland on the 18 July 1901 on the brig *Alert*.

Greenshield was heading into a grim wilderness of cold winters with violent continuous snowstorms, temperatures below zero Fahrenheit for over six months and coastal fog during the thaw season. It was reckoned that the Hudson Straits, which included eastern Baffin Island, had the worst climate of the Arctic with the heaviest snowfall, highest average windspeeds and the greatest number of days of summer fog. White men found the long hours of darkness particularly trying. Greenshield wrote: "There is not much in one's general surroundings to cheer or help or lift one up. The depth of winter, the short dull days, the long dark nights, all tend to depress . . ."

There was an austere beauty, too. Greenshield wrote in his diary: "A beautiful and calm day. The sun is now gaining strength and beginning to show himself for a short time above the rocky hills around about us, going down afterwards in a gold and purple glory which must be seen to be fully realised. . . . . . The Aurora shone with amazing splendour and brilliancy tonight, flashing up and down behind the hills, and trailing its long, mysterious fold-like beams of light across the sky overhead; and to its brilliancy later on was added the light of the moon as it gradually rose."

Greenshield arrived at the mission on Blacklead Island on 18 September and his first impression of his new home was of a bleak and inhospitable place. "The island looked a barren spot – not a bush, not a tree, not a blade of grass to be seen. Just a great greyish-brown mass." He spent two years there, learning to speak eskimo and putting his medical and practical skills to good use, caring for the sick and building the first hospital in the Arctic Circle – a one-roomed wooden hut at the mission!

In September 1903 Greenshield returned to England to finish his studies.

Having passed his examinations he was ordained deacon and, shortly after, hastily ordained priest in order to return to mission work. During his second spell in the Arctic from 1904–6, Greenshield took charge of the mission at Kikkerton, ten days's travel away from Blacklead Island. His own stature was growing and when the Rev Peck left on furlough he was put in charge of the mission on Blacklead Island for a year.

Back in England there was growing interest in the polar regions and on the Isle of Wight Greenshield found himself a minor celebrity and much in demand as a speaker. In December 1906 he lectured at Newport dressed in eskimo clothes and showed stuffed birds and animals, a model of a sledge outside an igloo with a typical eskimo family inside, and played a bloodcurdling phonograph of a bear-hunt followed by eskimo calls and incantations.

In 1908 Greenshield studied at the Livingstone Medical College for six months, work which was to prove invaluable to him. He received a letter from a young Scot who had applied to join Peck's missionary team and Greenshield wrote back of the joys of life in the Arctic. The letter was from A.L. Fleming, later Bishop of the Arctic, the famous Archibald the Arctic.

Following an uneventful third spell in the Arctic, Greenshield left Scotland on 30 July 1909 aboard the Dutch schooner *Jantina Agatha* on what proved to be a near disasterous fourth term in the Arctic wilderness. He wasn't the only passenger; the ship carried a famous German explorer who was going to Baffin Land to study Arctic bird life. On 25 September the ship's iron hull struck an iceberg lifting the bow clear of the water. The ship freed itself next day but as they steered towards land, which the Captain mistook for Blacklead Island, the ship began to sink.

Their situation was desperate. Of shipwrecks in the Arctic Greenshield said: "As a rule it makes little difference whether you go down with the ship. If you reach the coast you generally starve." They were thirty miles from land when the Captain gave the order to abandon ship. They loaded two boats and a skiff with stores (including the German's expedition stores), the Captain and four men in one boat, Greenshield and four men in the other.

For two days and nights they rowed the overloaded boats till they landed, exhausted, on a small rocky island. Greenshield decided that, if they were to survive, they must take one of the boats and attempt to reach Blacklead Island and organise a rescue. Greenshield and three others, including the Captain, left next day; under his skilful leadership they made the mission and picked up the remaining crew in the nick of time.

For the next eleven months they waged a grim battle against starvation; their stores would see one man through the winter, but there were ten of them! Greenshield made arduous trips to other missions and trading posts for stores, organised foraging parties when the stores were gone, helped cool tempers when things got ugly over the German's refusal to yield his stores, and kept morale high by keeping the men busy. When they were finally relieved by the arrival of the *Thomas* the Dutch crew were adamant that their survival was entirely down to Greenshield.

Greenshield arrived back in England a hero and celebrity. On a visit to the Isle of Wight he spoke to a crowd of 200 people crammed into the Leigh Richmond Hall eager to hear him recount his adventures. The Queen of the Netherlands was so moved by his tale that she made him a Knight of the Order of Orange-Nassau and granted him an allowance of 200 guilders to be spent on goods for the eskimos in honour of the "kindness displayed by them towards our shipwrecked mariners."

What of Greenshield's missionary zeal in bringing Christianity to the eskimo? Some observers would say that contact with the white man had proved wholly detrimental, that they learnt only vices from traders and missionaries. Yet there is no doubting that the eskimoes of Blacklead Island, Kikkerton and other missions had great affection and respect for Greenshield. The medical service he provided was exceptional considering the limitations and it was the work of Peck and Greenshield which lead to the establishment of St Luke's Hospital, Pangnirtung, the most northerly hospital in the world.

Greenshield's fifth and final journey to Blacklead Island, from 1911-13, called upon his medical skills to the utmost for there was much sickness among the eskimos and traders. At the end of his term the ship *Ernest William* was sent out to bring him home. Like many ships chartered by the Church Missionary Society, the *Ernest William* was unsuited to Arctic work and was trapped by ice and crushed. Greenshield, alert as ever, saw the ship was in difficulties and launched a boat to rescue the crew who were exhausted from working the pumps. Greenshield faced another *Jantina Agatha* situation, only worse. Luckily, a month later a small whaler came by which took him and the thankful crew back to England.

Back home Greenshield was at the height of his fame and embarked on a round of speaking engagements on behalf of the Church Missionary Society, the British and Foreign Bible Society and the Missions to Seamen. *The Christian World*, writing of the annual C.M.S. meeting in May 1914, stated: "One of the most popular speakers . . . has been the Rev E.W.T. Greenshield, the young CMS man, who has had so many stirring adventures in Baffin Land. He has a very deep voice and a rapid delivery pouring out story after story... he has vigorously championed the eskimos."

Greenshield's marriage to Jane Marion Kaye, a vicar's daughter, was widely reported in the Daily and Provincial press, the Daily Graphic dubbing him "Bishop of the Arctic." He longed to return to the Arctic but chose to look after his ailing parents instead, a fortuitious circumstance for the ship that would have taken him was lost with all hands. In 1917 he signed on as a Missions to Seamen Chaplain and spent the next five years ministering to sailors and fishermen in Ireland, the Shetlands and India. From 1922 till his death in 1938 he ran the Seamen's Mission in the depressed port of Middlesborough.

Greenshield was the rough and rugged sort, a man of action, a doer not a thinker, a man who could handle drunken sailors with ease and swap tales and share a smoke with hardy traders or eskimos. He was at ease among working men. He was happiest absorbed in the practical work of the mission, yet was zealous in proselytising the Faith. He was from a dying breed, an empire-builder with a simple belief in God, King and country. He was far different to the dogmatic, self-righteous, blinkered Victorian missionary though no less fervent in his belief in mission work. Today, in a world where religion plays a less central role in our lives, Edgar Greenshield seems old-fashioned, an anachronism – but those who knew him, never forgot him.

Remarkable Islanders

⁂ Admiral 'Snip' ⁂

Admiral Hopson

Many old guidebooks relate the story of Thomas Hopson, the orphan boy apprenticed to a tailor at Niton, who ran away to sea to join the navy. In his first sea battle he climbed the mast of the enemy's flagship and stole the flag, an action that won him the patronage of an admiral. Hopson rose rapidly through the ranks to become an admiral himself, nicknamed 'Snip,' and he made a surprise visit back to Niton to see the old tailor and his wife again. Though a popular story it is mostly fabrication, but the truth behind his career is just as fascinating.

Very little is known of Hopson's early life but one version states he was born in 1643 to Captain Anthony Hopson and his wife, Ann, of Shalfleet. The family was in reduced circumstances; local tradition has it that young Thomas ran away to sea and he was certainly serving in the navy by 1666. He was second lieutenant on the *Dreadnought* by 1672 and on 21 March 1678 Admiral Herbert, commanding the Mediterranean Fleet, commissioned him captain of the *Tiger Prize*. Herbert wrote of Hopson he had "as much merit as modesty, and so much of both that . . . any man when he becomes well known will be proud to have been the instrument of his preferment."

Hopson went on to captain a succession of ships and fought in the battle of Beachy Head and the battle of Barfleur. In 1693 he hoisted his Admiral's pennant aboard the *Breda* and the following year was promoted Vice Admiral of the Blue. Much of that summer was spent trying to trap the great French seaman, Jean Bart's squadron in the channel and off Dunkirk. In a naval career spanning forty years Thomas Hopson took part in forty-two engagements, the last of which, the Battle of Vigo Bay, was also his greatest triumph.

Vigo Bay was a major Anglo-Dutch victory at the beginning of the War of the Spanish Succession. In 1702 Hopson was serving as Vice-Admiral under Sir George Rooke who led a powerful fleet and army against Cadiz in July. It was a miserable failure. On the voyage home Rooke learnt that the Spanish treasure fleet that had left Havana in July for Europe, escorted by a French squadron under Chateaurenault, had arrived in Vigo Bay on the Galician coast. The French admiral at once began strengthening local defences and laid a strong boom across the entrance to Redondela harbour. Rooke decided that here was an opportunity to make amends for his failure at Cadiz.

On 12 October 1702 Hopson, in the 80-gun *Torbay*, led the Anglo-Dutch line of battle into the harbour, the *Torbay* making all sail to break the boom. With the boom pierced troops were landed to take the batteries and a fierce action then followed in the Bay. Hopson's flagship engaged the *Bourbon* and the *Esperance* before a fireship set her foresail alight. The fireship, a commandeered merchant vessel packed with snuff, exploded and her cargo put out the flames but almost blinded and suffocated those that were near. With his ship shattered and 115 of his men killed, Hopson transferred to the *Monmouth* and continued to command. A monument to Hopson at Weybridge records that he forced the boom "with his usual resolution and conduct, whereby he made way for the whole confederate fleet to enter, take and destroy all the enemy's ships of war and galleons." Twenty-one French and Spanish warships and twenty lesser craft were taken or destroyed and some booty captured for which Hopson rightly received most of the credit.

On 29 November 1702, upon his return to England, Hopson was knighted and appointed a commissioner of the navy with a salary of £500 per annum, in recognition of his good work. He remained a commissioner until 1714, served as Governor of Greenwich Hospital for four years and as colonel of the eastern regiment of the Cinque Ports militia. He was also Member of Parliament for Newtown for seven years (1698 – 1705) but rarely took part in proceedings.

Thomas Hopson was highly regarded by most of the leading admirals of the day with whom he served – Herbert, Russell and Rooke. He was a compassionate commander and in 1702 begged for the life of a captain, condemned to be shot for cowardice because "when I was a youth in the Isle of Wight, (I remember) that his father had the character of a very loyal gentleman . . . he is ancient, and has an ancient wife, and (I beg) that they may see each other before they die."

BATTLE OF VIGO BAY, 1702

Remarkable Islanders

THE WOEFUL WOODVILLES

Elizabeth Woodville

The Woodville's of Northampton were not one of the kingdom's great noble families, but for one generation they appear on the stage of English history. The rise of the family was meteoric, their demise equally swift and tragic. During their brief ascendancy two of the Woodvilles, Anthony and Edward, were governors of the Isle of Wight; both, in their way, were responsible for calamities.

Anthony Woodville, Earl Rivers, was known for his gallantry in the field and his love of literature, a wielder of the pen as well as the sword, a quixotic knight errant whose love of jousting, crusades and pilgrimages places him in a waning age of chivalry. Immortalised by Shakespeare in *Richard III*, Earl Rivers went to his death "For truth, for duty, and for loyalty" as protector of the Prince of Wales, murdered with his brother in the Tower. Edward Woodville, a bold but rash adventurer, was responsible for the worst catastrophe for island arms, leading some four hundred men from the Isle of Wight to their deaths in Brittany.

The Woodvilles came to prominence when King Edward IV fell under the spell of Elizabeth Woodville, widow of a Lancastrian knight. Edward was out hunting and his party rested overnight at a castle. Elizabeth, niece of the owner, was staying there and Edward was charmed by her. She and her two sons were under the ban of the attainder which disinherited the adherents of Lancaster, after the Wars of the Roses. Elizabeth saw here an opportunity to advance her family by winning the King's favour and obtaining royal mercy.

The romance flourished which worried Richard Neville, Earl of Warwick, known as the 'Kingmaker', for it was he and his compatriots that had put Edward on the throne. They had plans for a diplomatic marriage to a French

EARL RIVERS

princess as part of their foreign policy. But Edward married Elizabeth in secret at Grafton on 1 May 1464 and only revealed this union to Warwick and others some five months later. The following year she was crowned Queen Consort at Westminster.

Elizabeth had five brothers, seven sisters and two sons and by royal decree Edward raised them to high rank or married them into great families. Her father, Richard Woodville, was made treasurer of the kingdom and created Lord Rivers. One brother, Sir John Woodville, was married to the dowager duchess of Norfolk, though she was old enough to be his grandmother. Her second eldest brother, Anthony, married the daughter of Lord Scales, believed to be the wealthiest heiress in the country. In 1467 the king granted to "Anthony Wydeville, knight, Lord Scales, in special tail, viz. to his heirs male the whole Island of Wight with the Castle of Carisbrooke and all other hereditaments by fealty for all services."

The aggrandisement of the Woodvilles, with eight new peerages coming to the family at a time when there were but sixty peers of the realm, was both an affront and a danger to Warwick. By 1470 he'd had enough and rebelled; in the ensuing turmoil Warwick beheaded Elizabeth's father, Richard Woodville, Lord Rivers, and her brother John Woodville. With his father and elder brother dead, Anthony took the title Earl Rivers. Warwick himself was later killed, battered to death at the Battle of Barnet.

Anthony was a deeply religious man and his piety prompted him to translate *The Dictes and Sayings of the Philosophers*, for the instruction of his nephew, the young Prince of Wales. He became a patron of Thomas Caxton and Woodville's *Dictes* was the first book to be printed in England. Other translations from the French included the "wise and wholesome" *Proverbs of Christine de Pisan* and the *Cordyal*, each printed by Caxton. In a manuscript copy of one of these translations there is an illustration in which the Earl is depicted introducing Caxton to Edward IV, his Queen and the Prince. A parvenu poet and man of letters, the literary endeavours of this 'amiable lord,' as Horace Walpole called him, were mediocre; Walpole included the *Dictes* in his list of very dull books!

In 1467, Edward IV had plans to marry off his sister Margaret to Charles, Count of Charolais and future Duke of Burgundy, who commissioned Anthony, the Bastard of Burgundy, to negotiate the marriage on his behalf. Woodville had challenged Anthony two years previously but the tournament between Burgundy's emissary and Anthony Woodville didn't finally take place until 11/12 June 1467 at Smithfield. The noblest knights from all England, Scotland and the Continent assembled before the King, eager to watch the outcome of the combat, which excited great expectations.

On the first day they fought on horseback and the Burgundian's horse was killed. On the second day they fought with axes and Woodville acquitted himself well and the joust was declared drawn. According to one English chronicler the contest ended without wound or bloodshed to either combatant. Next year at the marriage of Margaret to the Duke of Burgundy, Anthony broke eleven lances in a contest with Adolf of Cleves.

Anthony was the military specialist at the Yorkist court and if it wasn't for his predilection for crusades and pilgrimages, which undoubtedly hampered his career, his influence under Edward IV would have been greater. He fought and was wounded at Towton and the following year, 1468, was appointed commander of a naval force to aid Brittany against France. In 1472 he took a relieving force to Brittany and took part in Edward's invasion of France in 1475. But he also found time during these years to fight the Saracens in Portugal, for a pilgrimage to Santiago de Compostela and to visit the holy places of Italy.

The death of Edward IV in 1483, with the Prince of Wales a boy of twelve, left the king's brother, Richard of Gloucester, as Protector of the kingdom during the minority. These were anxious times for the Woodvilles who were still much detested by the old nobility. The Woodvilles wanted government by council with Richard as chief councillor. Richard had no intention of sharing power and saw it as essential that the queen "a busy and negotiating woman" and her ambitious family were removed from the direction of affairs for they were in powerful positions.

The queen's son by her first marriage, the Marquis of Dorset, was Constable of the Tower in charge of Edward IV's treasure. Sir Edward Woodville, the queen's brother, was in command of the fleet, ready for immediate duty. But above all Edward, heir to the throne, was at Ludlow Castle under the care and protection of his uncle, Anthony Woodville, Lord Rivers. When the queen sent for them to come to London, she was so worried for the young prince's safety that she insisted on an escort of 2,000 men.

They were met at Stony Stratford by Richard of Gloucester and the Duke of Buckingham. Rivers suspected nothing untoward at this and dined with them that evening. The next morning he was arrested and sent northward under heavy guard to Pontefract Castle. When the queen was informed she fled with her family to the Sanctuary at Westminster. When Richard of Gloucester reached London he had both young princes confined to the Tower. The queen's marriage to Edward IV was declared null and void and the princes bastardised. Their fate was sealed when Richard took the throne as King Richard III.

On 23 June 1483 Anthony Earl Rivers and his associates were beheaded at Pontefract Castle without any form of trial. The execution was public and the victims were prevented from addressing the crowd. As a lover of literature Anthony Woodville would have been pleased with his death in the hands of Shakespeare for he selflessly prays "Be satisfied, dear God, with our true blood" and save his "sister and her princely sons" *(Act III Scene iii)*.

The Woodvilles were not completely neutralised until Sir Edward, in command of the fleet anchored off the Kent coast, was rendered harmless. News was spread of a general pardon for all sailors and the fleet broke up, leaving Edward with just two ships in which he made good his escape to Brittany to the Tudor's court in exile. With the victory of Henry Tudor in 1485, Edward Woodville was rewarded with the Castle and Lordship of the Isle of Wight.

In 1488 Edward Woodville undertook to raise a force from the island to assist the Duke of Brittany against the King of France. When King Henry VII refused his support for the venture Edward went ahead regardless thinking no doubt he had Henry's tacit connivance. In a general muster of island arms Woodville selected forty gentlemen and four hundred "from the stoutest of the commonalty;" the soldiers wore white coats with the red cross embroided upon them. They set sail from St Helens in four ships and en route to Brittany they plundered a French vessel.

They landed at St Malo and joined the Duke of Brittany's forces. The Breton leaders were glad of assistance and, in order to exploit the prestige of the English bowmen, they dressed 1,300 of their own men in jerkins bearing the cross of St George. On the 20 July 1488, between Andouille and Saint Aubins-du-Cormier, they engaged the French army in a general fight. The French, under their commander La Tremouille, won a complete victory; in military terms it was men against boys, for the French had field artillery and gunpowder against the island levies armed with pikes, bows and arrows. No quarter was given to the English and Sir Edward Woodville and all his followers except one boy were slain. The boy returned to the Isle of Wight to deliver the news of the slaughter.

With the death of Edward, the woeful Woodvilles disappear from history, both national and local, and return to the obscurity from whence they came. Anthony was governor of the island from 1466-1483; during his governorship, he completed the second entrance to Carisbrooke Castle. This notable gatehouse, flanked by twin, castellated towers, with portcullis and bold embrasures, bears for posterity Anthony's coat of arms, a Yorkist rose on either side, cut into a stone of the parapet. Of Edward, governor from 1485-1488, no evidence remains.

Remarkable Islanders

⁂ Prisoner Of Conscience ⁂

Philip Bagwell, Ventnor Councillor, 1930

War makes ordinary men and women do extraordinary things. In the ugly turmoil of bloody conflict they conquer fear to perform feats of outstanding bravery and self-sacrifice. We put them on a pedestal as heroes of nation and empire, shining examples for us to emulate. But what do we make of a man who, through the courage of his convictions, refuses to go to war, against the drift of public opinion, against the demands of national citizenship, against the power of state compulsion; who risks his family, his livelihood and his social reputation and endures instead the rigours of imprisonment? Is he not, in his way, a hero too?

Philip William Bagwell was born in Sevenoaks, Kent on 29 March 1885. At 16 he went to work for a firm of auctioneers in Tenterden and when, a year later, his father died Philip, out of necessity, took charge of the family. It was another four years before he came of age and during this time he formed firm political and religious ideas. He read Christian newspapers, devoured all the campaigning books of the day and listened ardently to the sermons delivered at many different nonconformist churches. He believed that religion was about more than the salvation of individual souls; it was relevant to our everyday lives and could not be divorced from political action.

Philip became a keen advocate of temperance, slum clearances and municipal housing. He was a life-long opponent of betting (especially on horses) and a dedicated advocate of keeping Sunday special. The Rev James Barr's five lectures entitled *Christianity and War*, published in 1901/2 argued the case for pacifism and greatly influenced Philip's own attitude to war.

On the 10 December 1906, at the age of 21, Philip bought the Newsagents and Stationers at 74, High Street, Ventnor. Apart from the period of his imprisonment, he lived and worked here for the next fifty-two years, until he sold the business in 1958, just a week before he died. While working in Tenterden Philip met Nellie Aldrich but it wasn't until June 1910, when family matters were settled and he grew confident in his new business, that he felt sure enough of his future to get married.

For the next few years, as Europe stumbled from crisis to crisis towards war, Philip's political and religious views became increasingly pacifist and collectivist. He read the sermons of R. J. Campbell, leader of the 'New Theology' movement, in *The Christian Commonwealth* in which Campbell declared himself a socialist. Disgusted with the Liberal Government for their secret diplomacy and sponsorship of rearmament, Philip joined the Independent Labour Party and proudly hung a framed photo of Keir Hardie on his office wall. The party's weekly newspaper, *The Labour Leader*, was avidly read.

When war came in August 1914 Britain, alone among the European nations, had no conscript army. The principle of a professional army based on voluntary enlistment was etched deep into the national consciousness; it was part of our civil liberties. From 1660 to 1916 war was the concern of the professional soldier. Lord Salisbury boasted at the end of the Boer War that the Boers had been defeated by soldiers attracted to the army "not by coercion but by the emoluments and the honours of a great and splendid vocation."
A compact, professional army was adequate for Britain's small colonial wars but a European conflagration would mean total war, the whole nation mobilised. Kitchener told the War Council on the first day of war, "we must be prepared to put armies of millions in the field and maintain them for several years." In November 1914 the No Conscription Fellowship was set up amid growing fears that compulsion was on the way. It described itself as "an

organisation of men likely to be called upon to undertake military service in the event of conscription, who will refuse from conscientious motives to bear arms, because they consider human life to be sacred and cannot therefore assume the responsibility of inflicting death." Philip became a member in June 1915.

By mid 1915 the war on the western front was swallowing men at a rate the voluntary system could not cope with. Neither Kitchener's famous recruiting campaign nor Lord Derby's scheme were mustering enough men. Until the National Registration Act of July 1915 nobody even knew how many men were available for military service. Conscription finally arrived with the Military Service Acts of January and June 1916 under which both single and married men between the ages of 18 and 41 were deemed liable to military service. Local tribunals were set up to hear applications for exemption and were instructed to give due consideration "to the man whose objection genuinely rests on religious and moral convictions."

The Acts allowed an applicant exemption from combatant service if he was prepared "to undertake work of national importance." When Philip appeared before the local tribunal in June 1916 he followed the 'absolutist' line of the NCF; he would not fight and neither would he aid and abet the war effort in any way. His application was turned down, and so were his appeals; on 12 January 1916 Philip Bagwell entered Wormwood Scrubbs Prison under military escort and, as prisoner number 2685, began a 56-day term of imprisonment under harsh conditions, much of it spent in solitary confinement sewing mailbags.

He was released on 24 February into the care of the army and returned to his unit. He refused to accept military orders and was court-martialled receiving a second term in gaol of five months from March to August 1917. He was jailed a third time, swiftly following his release, this time for two years with hard labour. Altogether Philip spent 27 months in gaol during which time he had the unstinting support of his wife Nellie, who was quick to scotch any suggestion from the shop's customers that she did not share her husband's views!

Back home at Ventnor the local community was sharply divided over its opinion of Philip Bagwell. "There are people in Ventnor who would hang Mr Bagwell," said the editor of the *Isle of Wight Mercury* who went on to praise his "character, ability and independence." This division was abundantly clear when Philip stood for election to Ventnor Urban District Council in 1924. A few yards from Philip's shop two shopkeepers slung a banner across the street reading 'Vote to keep the conchy out.' A crowd of over a thousand people, nearly half the electorate for the ward, assembled outside the town hall to hear the result, Philip's supporters near the front and those hostile to him at the back. A reporter present noted "There was a distinct pause before Mr Bagwell's name was given out. When the company heard it there was very loud cheering from a body of people right in front of the Town Hall entrance, while from the back came a good deal of booing." Philip was elected and went on to serve as a councillor for 24 years and twice coming top of the poll, in 1929 and 1936.

Philip's courageous stance on the war and his well-argued convictions earnt him the deep respect even of his opponents. The editor of the *Isle of Wight Mercury*, Mr Barton W. Russell, reporting the hearings of the tribunal, found Philip's standpoint untenable and illogical yet was moved to admit "his reasons were invariably distinct, clear and evidently well weighed and well considered. There is not the slightest doubt as to the inherent sincerity of his convictions

The shop at 74, High Street, Ventnor

which were argued with potency and courage." When Philip sought election to the local council, heading the nomination paper as proposer was Mr Fred Baker who, as Chairman of the Ventnor Tribunal, had turned down Philip's application for exemption from military service! It is truly extraordinary for a man to win over his opponents over an issue so bitterly divisive as war.

Remarkable Islanders

⁂ The Dragon Hunter ⁂

POLACANTHUS FOXII

Brighstone proudly boasts that three of its rectors became bishops – there was Bishop Ken, 'Soapy Sam' Wilberforce and Bishop Moberly, all remembered in the name of the local pub, The Three Bishops. But who remembers the humble curate riding out to the coast on his donkey to search the crumbling cliffs for "terrible lizards", returning home at dusk along the narrow country lanes, laden down with his latest finds? Yet the Rev William D. Fox probably discovered more species of dinosaur than anyone else in the UK and has more dinosaurs named after him than any other Englishman. His impact on the study and discovery of British dinosaurs is almost unparalleled!

Fox was born in Cumberland, the son of a yeoman farmer, and a batchelor all his life. He arrived on the Isle of Wight in 1862 to take up the post of curate of Brighstone Church at the age of 43. For most of his life on the island he lodged at Myrtle Cottage, next door to the old Post Office (now the Village Museum), in the centre of the village and with the coastline within easy reach. Fox was no professional scientist but an avid amateur collector of fossils. He rarely attempted to write about his discoveries, preferring to leave that to those he regarded as the experts, although on occasion he did submit notes to magazines like *Athenaeum* and *Geological Magazine* and sometimes to scientific meetings e.g. of the British Association for the Advancement of Science.

Perhaps Fox spent too much time looking for dinosaurs and not enough on his work for his own good. This was certainly the opinion of Mrs McCall, wife of the vicar of Brighstone, who said of Fox, "It was always the bones first and the parish next." When Fox's position as curate was under threat he wrote to Sir Richard Owen (who was first to use the term 'dinosaur', meaning "terrible lizard") asking for his support to remain in his post, pointing out the valuable contributions he had made to scientific discovery whilst on the island. Fox wrote, "I cannot leave this place while I have any money left to live on, I take such deep (joy) in hunting for old dragons." Despite writing to the Prime Minister, Gladstone, Owen was unable to secure his job, and in 1874 Fox became curate to Kingston parish, and remained on the island till his death in 1881.

Fox was friendly with Alfred Lord Tennyson, who took a great interest in natural history, and kept company with some of the most distinguished scientists of the day. Owen was known to have visited Fox on at least one occasion and may even have collected fossils with him. Fox kept up a correspondence with

Owen particularly over the new discovery of dinosaur bones. It is likely, too, that John Hulke, who became President of the Geological Society, collected fossils with Fox, too.

In 1865 Fox discovered a partial skeleton of the armoured dinosaur polacanthus, a herbivore up to five metres long, with a low arched profile and an array of spines for protection. The first bones of this dinosaur, collected from Sandown in 1843, were left in a hackney carriage and lost. Fox's was the first and remains the only substantial specimen of this dinosaur, although there is a privately owned partial skeleton on display in Martin Simpson's Fossil Shop at Blackgang Chine. The name 'polacanthus' was proposed by Owen at a meeting of the British Association for the Advancement of Science in 1864; he also wrote anonymously in the *Illustrated London News* of 16 September 1865 suggesting 'foxii' as the specific name for this new Wealden dinosaur in honour of Fox's discovery.

Fox was not the first to discover the small, bipedal herbivore, hysilophodon; the first specimen was found by workmen at Cowleaze Chine and passed on to, among others, Gideon Mantell, who thought it was just a juvenile iguanodon. However, Fox found another skeleton in the same place and wrote to Richard Owen suggesting there were significant differences with iguanodon and that it should be treated as a separate species. Fox was right and Thomas Huxley, when describing the dinosaur in 1869, proposed 'hysilophodon foxii' in honour of Fox's contribution.

Two other dinosaurs, aristosuchus and calamospondylus, were discovered by Fox and, in the case of the latter, his finds remain the only known specimens. These two species were at first confused but Fox wrote to Owen stating the two were different beasts; Fox's description of calamospondylus in the *Athenaeum* and also *Geological Magazine* made this clear. It was Fox who created the name, his suggestion first appearing in a letter to Owen.

When William D. Fox died in 1881 his large collection of fossils, numbering more than 500 specimens, was acquired by the British Museum where it is still housed and continues to provide valuable insights into a past world. It is ironic that the curate from Brighstone should have contributed so much to a science that was helping to tear up the traditional doctrines of the Church, not least the story of Creation, though it was the Church that paid his humble wages. He was buried in the graveyard at Brighstone; his gravestone lies just a few metres south of the church entrance, marked by a simple stone cross.

Remarkable Islanders

⚜ The Queen Of Chantilly ⚜

SOPHIE DAWES

If success in life is judged by how far you travel from your origins then Sophie Dawes's life must be judged an unqualified success. The smugglers daughter from St Helens became the mistress of Louis Henri Joseph, Duc de Bourbon, the last of the Condés and held sway over him for twenty years. Notorious and much talked about in the salons of France, she was Queen of Chantilly to some, and the uncomplimentary 'Montespan de Saint-Leu' to others. She was intelligent and ambitious and, according to one observer, "a person of very extraordinary talents; her history is the greatest romance of real life within my knowledge."

Sophie Dawes was born in St Helens in 1792, daughter of fisherman and infamous smuggler, Dickie Dawes. When she was 10 her father died and the family went to the workhouse at Parkhurst, unable to cope. At 15 she ran away to Portsmouth, then to London, taking a variety of jobs which included selling oranges outside Covent Garden Theatre. With luck and guile she captivated an Army officer and became his mistress; he established her in a house at Turnham Green and bought her an annuity of £50, scarcely enough to pay her milliner's bill once she became accustomed to spending.

Sophie was ambitious, mixing with the higher social classes, and became determined to exploit her 'assets' to the full. She became the mistress of the exiled Duc de Bourbon in 1811 when he allegedly won her from the Duke of Kent in a game of cards. The Duc was delighted with Sophie and he took a house for Sophie and her mother in Gloucester Street, Queen's Square. He paid for her education, engaging the best teachers, and in three years she had mastered Greek, Latin and music and could read and write fluently in French. The Duc was most generous to Sophie and gave her 20,000 francs (£800) a year as pin-money.

After a breach with the Duc of some years Sophie moved to Paris, hoping to effect a reconciliation, waiting patiently for him to tire of his latest English mistress, Mrs Harris. Eventually, the Duc agreed to restore her position so long as she went under another name; in effect, he wanted Sophie married and so a search began for a 'suitable' husband. He was found in the person of Adrien Victor de Feucheres, an officer in the Royal Guards and credulous enough to please everyone. They married in London on 16 August 1818; the following year he was given the title of baron and made aide-de-camp to his wife's lover. The *ménage a trios* took up residence at Chantilly and for four years the baron, believing Sophie to be the Duc's daughter, was blind to her real role.

Estrangement from her husband and the death of the Duc's wife placed Sophie openly at the head of the Duc's household and she used her position shamelessly; she tried to persuade the Duc to alter his will in her favour and she looked after her own family by securing them favours. She was not popular with the French people, because she was English and haughty in manner; her carriage was stoned and she was hissed and booed at the theatre, but this did nothing to dilute her flaunted ambition.

In the spring of 1829 Sophie persuaded the aging Duc to give her one of his most treasured possessions, the forest of Enghien, worth 100,000 francs (£4,000) a year. The Duc, ill and alone, having survived both his wife and only son, pondered who to leave his considerable fortune to. Sophie, in league with the Duc d'Orleans, remorselessly bullied the old man for years to sign a will which divided his fortune between Sophie and the Duc d'Orleans son, to whom the Duc de Bourbon was godfather. Tired of the bickering, on 30 August 1829 the Duc signed a will making the Duc d'Aumale, his godson, his residuary legatee and bequeathing a fortune of fourteen million francs to his "faithful companion, Mme la baronne de Feucheres," together with the chateaux and estates of Saint Leu-Taverny, Boissy, Enghien, Montmorency and Mortefontaine, the pavilion in the Palais-Bourbon and all his furniture, carriages, horses etc. In July 1830 France was once more plunged into revolutionary turmoil and the Duc de Bourbon feared the return of the uncertain days of 1793. He made half-hearted plans to leave France and escape both the political situation and the machinations of his scheming mistress. But, on the morning of 27 August 1830, the Duc was found hanging by his handerkerchief from the *espagnolette* of the long French window in his bedroom. Few people believed in the suicide theory; most people believed he was murdered and the public, encouraged by the press, suspected Sophie's involvement. After all, she stood to benefit from his will.

When Charles X went into exile and Louis-Philippe, Duc d'Orleans, ascended the throne of France, Sophie received royal protection against prosecution and was admitted to the court from which she had been barred for so long. But even the new king and his queen soon abandoned Sophie when she became too much of an embarrassment. When things got too hot in France Sophie sold the chateaux she was bequeathed and returned to England. She bought the estate of Bure Homage in Hampshire and a house at 5 Hyde Park Square, London. She always saw her family was well looked after and gave money away to charity. Towards the end of 1839 her health began to fail and she died a year later on 15 December 1840 of an attack of angina. She showed no sign of fear at approaching death; it is said that, standing at her bedside, Sir Astley Cooper, the most eminent surgeon of his day, whispered to her nephew, Edward Dawes, "She dies game." A fitting epitaph indeed!

It was Sophie's fate to be born in a fisherman's cottage, brought up in the workhouse, live in a palace and die young, before she had a chance to really enjoy her prince's millions. How should we remember her then? The poor girl who rose from rags to riches by guile and ambition? Or the brothel-girl and mistress, the gold-digger who murdered an old man for his millions. The tablet over the cottage door in St Helens makes no judgment and says only that "Sophie Dawes . . . known as the Queen of Chantilly, was born here about 1792."

Duc de Bourbon

Remarkable Islanders

ENGLAND'S LEONARDO

TELESCOPE INVENTED BY HOOKE

Robert Hooke was one of the most brilliant and versatile of seventeenth century English scientists. His speculations ranged over the whole field of natural philosophy "from the minutest disclosures of the microscope to the furthest sweep of the telescope," and he left his mark on almost every scientific and mechanical project of his day. The diversity of his accomplishments is impressive: intuitive and gifted scientist and scientific artist, tenacious debater, instrument designer of genius and first rate architect, surveyor and developer. He was a true renaissance man, England's equivalent to the fourteenth century genius Leonardo da Vinci. Yet his persona and achievements were overshadowed by rivals like Sir Isaac Newton (with whom he was engaged in bitter controversy) and Sir Christopher Wren.

This was partly Hooke's own fault for "his Temper was Melancholy, Mistrustful and Jealous" which made him an object of dislike in his own day. Hooke is described by Richard Waller, his biographer, as small and crooked, "very pale and lean . . . his nose but thin . . . his chin sharp. . . He wore his own hair . . . very long and hanging neglected over his face uncut and lank." Isaac Asimov summarizes the standard opinion of Hooke as "a nasty, argumentative individual, anti-social, miserly, and quarrelsome" who took a "malignant pleasure in controversy" and thus always unlikely to be a candidate for the acclaim of posterity.

Even Freshwater, where Robert's father, John Hooke, was curate, seems to have forgotten Robert Hooke for the little museum devoted to him has now closed. It was in the rectory that Robert was born on 18 July 1635. He was a puny, weak child and not expected to live, but he had a keen intellect and was always asking questions. He amused himself by inventing curious toys like a wooden clock and a model ship with guns which fired. At 13 his father died and he was taken in by Dr Busby of Westminster School where he mastered ancient languages. He went on to Christ Church College, Oxford where he met many of those, like Robert Boyle and Christopher Wren, who would go on to form the Royal Society. Hooke lived in exciting times. Science was breaking new ground with its emphasis on practical experiment rather than the speculative philosophy at the heart the Aristotlean system. Hooke's hero,

Sir Francis Bacon, championed the cause of experiment, remarking that nature must be 'put to the torture' if its secrets were to be revealed. The torture chamber was the laboratory and the tools of persuasion were newly invented scientific instruments.

As a designer and inventor of such instruments Robert Hooke was unrivalled in his day. He invented the compound microscope, built the first reflecting telescope and designed a marine telescope. In horology his inventions include the anchor escapement of clocks, spring control of the balance wheel in watches and a 'weather clock.' Hooke's universal joint is found in all motor vehicles today. His other inventions include a wheel barometer, an odometer, an anemometer, a reflecting and a screw-divided quadrant.

Nothing, from the nature of light and the origin of fossils to the rotation of the planets and the lifecycle of the flea, escaped his enquiring eye. Hooke's *Micrographia*, published in 1665, was the result of observations and experiments between 1661 and 1664 using magnifying lenses, the objects of study ranging from a flea to lunar craters. It was brilliant in its wide-ranging investigations; his work on cellular structure based on studies of cork lead to discussions on the role of air in combustion; an anatomical description of a fly became an essay on aerodynamics and acoustics. In his *Attempt to Prove the Motion of the Earth* (1674) he expounded a theory of planetary motion and his interest in gravity would occupy him for 20 years.

Newton's *Discourse on Colour* provoked objections from Hooke on the grounds that "the main of it was contained in *Micrographia*." If Hooke was cantankerous in defending his work, Newton was bitterly resentful of any criticism. Publication of Newton's *Principia* brought fresh claims from Hooke;

in fact, so great was Newton's irritation at Hooke's objections that he delayed his *Opticks* until after Hooke's death. Less well known is Hooke's career as an architect yet he was appointed Surveyor by the City of London following the Great Fire of 1666 and designed many London buildings, few of which survived Victorian redevelopment and the Blitz. The Royal College of Physicians is gone and so is the Bethlehem Hospital, known as 'Bedlam.' He worked with Wren on the design of the Royal Observatory Greenwich and The Monument to the great fire in Fish Hill Street.

Robert's brother, John Hooke, had a daughter called Grace who became Robert's housekeeper in London. However, there is more than a suggestion that Grace's true role was that of common law wife to Robert and when she died in 1687 he was deeply affected. Perhaps it was the discovery that Robert was sleeping with his daughter that drove John, a former Mayor of Newport, to hang himself. Whatever the truth, Hooke's last years were dogged by ill health, possibly the result of diabetes, and he died lonely, sick and blind in 1703.

The breadth of his knowledge and researches, from physics to physiology, was the result of his search for a 'grand unified theory' to bind the whole of nature together. If the grand theory eluded him, so did recognition of his comprehensive genius until recent years. It seems a cruel twist of fate that, whereas the image of Newton illuminates his achievements, no portrait has survived to redeem Hooke from the shadow of history and the memorial window at Bishopsgate depicting Hooke was destroyed in the London bombings; his remains, lost since they were exhumed and reburied 'somewhere in North London', have foiled plans by experts in facial reconstruction to give Robert Hooke a face. And so he must remain visually anonymous, a man without a face to give expression to his character and intelligence.

Remarkable Islanders
The Moralising Maid

Elizabeth Missing Sewell

The photograph in the front of Elizabeth Missing Sewell's autobiography shows a small, stout woman with a prominent nose and lips, a rather prim and proper lady. The novelist Mary Crawford Fraser, who attended Sewell's school, recalled "her narrow but staunch religious beliefs" and "decorous lawfulness in every detail of the conduct of life." Elizabeth Sewell was the embodiment of Victorian moral and religious values, a prolific and popular authoress of more than fifty novels and educational books, whose lifelong interest was the moral and academic education of young middle class girls.

Elizabeth was born on 19 February 1815 at High Street, Newport. She was part of a large family of twelve children, seven sons and five daughters. Their father, Newport solicitor Thomas Sewell, lost over £3,000 in two bank failures and died in 1842 leaving the family encumbered by debt. Rather than declare insolvency the family undertook to pay off all debts and repay all creditors, a task that took the best part of thirty years. Elizabeth was educated at Newport and Bath from where she returned home early to help with the education of her younger sisters. Thus began her interest in girls' education.

The earnings from Elizabeth's writing were to become an essential means of financial support to the family. Her first publication, of which her brother William was editor, was *Stories, Illustrative of the Lords Prayer*. Her novels, intended for a female readership, examined the spiritual and domestic anxieties of young girls and were extremely popular in America as well as Britain. The scrupulous observance of moral principle was Sewell's main preoccupation; her novels included *Amy Herbert* (1844), *Gertrude* (1845) and *Laneton Parsonage* (1846-8).

The moral rectitude of the Victorian middle class, which Elizabeth Sewell represented, is partly explained as a reaction to the regency and reign of

George IV, an era of moral degeneration whereby a slovenly, self-indulgent monarch set new standards in low behaviour – gambling, womanising and drinking the monarchy into debt. Her brother William, tutor and scholar, was a great influence and through him she met leading members of the Oxford Movement which sought to revitalise the Church of England by reviving traditional Catholic doctrines and rituals. Elizabeth firmly believed in the need for middle class girls to be given clear moral training in Church of England principles.

In 1852 Elizabeth started a school at the family home in Bonchurch, called Ashcliff, and her nieces were the first pupils. In 1866 she began St Boniface School, Ventnor. She believed all children should have a broad historical education and wrote several textbooks for schools including her *Historical Selections* (1868). Elizabeth had travelled abroad and met such prominent literary figures as Wordsworth and Browning, and Tennyson and Swinburne nearer home, but despite this widening experience she remained deeply conservative. While other prominent Victorian ladies were seeking to free women from domestic dictatorship, Elizabeth continued to believe woman's place was in the home and education should prepare girls for domestic life.

Her final novel *Home and After Life* was published in 1891 but she was no longer a popular authoress. Elizabeth survived all her sisters and was supported in her old age by an annuity from grateful pupils and an award of £300 from the Royal Literary Fund. She died at home on 17 August 1906.

Ashcliff in Bonchurch

Remarkable Islanders

The Natural Historian

When he was just a small boy, Frank Morey decided to compile a list of all the animals in the world. He began with lion, tiger, elephant and all went well until his older sister said she was sure there was more than one kind of deer and more than one kind of antelope. Then someone declared that, although it could fly, a bat was not a bird. Young Frank, thoroughly confused, decided to postpone his project until he knew more about natural history.

Over the next twenty years he devoted most of his scant leisure time to the study of entomology and other subjects, in the process amassing collections of natural history objects, including 2-3,000 insects, shells and plants together with data on their habitats and localities. These records were to form the nucleus of his *Guide to the Natural History of the Isle of Wight*, a bold attempt to bring together all the island's treasures in one volume. It was the culmination of a life's work which began with that boyhood list.

When Morey's *Guide* was published in 1909 it was by a long way the most comprehensive account of the natural history of a well-defined area of considerable size in the country. He brought together the work of a remarkable number of people, drawing on their records, collections and observations, their expertise in identification and specialist knowledge to compile lists of species and to write introductory articles.

In defence of the accusation that his *Guide* was a 'dry' list of questionable usefulness, Morey argued that one of the chief objects of studying natural history is to trace the distribution of the various species which can only be done by the making of local lists. "One is inclined to ask of an animal or plant in any given district, in Charles Kingsley's words, 'How did you get here? By what road did you come? What was your last place of abode? And now you are here, how do you get your living? Are you and your children thriving, or growing pauperised and degraded and dying out?'"

Frank Morey was born on 4 March 1858, one of the sons of H.W. Morey, founder of the firm of timber merchants. He became a dedicated amateur naturalist in the tradition of Gilbert White and his personal knowledge of island flora and fauna was immense. He was elected Fellow of the Linnean Society in 1906 and was an active member of many other bodies including the Selborne Society, the British Association, the Geologists Association and the Anthropological Institute. He had travelled extensively in France, northern Europe, India, Ceylon, Egypt and Palestine and harvested a store of interesting facts in the course of these travels. He at once appreciated that his *Guide* would need updating with supplementary lists as new records and localities were discovered. So in 1919 he founded the Isle of Wight Natural History Society, taking on the role of Secretary and Editor of *Proceedings* in which he intended publishing such lists.

From 1912 he acted as Honorary Curator of the Archaeological Museum at Carisbrooke Castle and he took on the task of organising the fossil collection for the newly created Isle of Wight Museum of Geology located at the Sandown Free Library. All this work he took on because of his underlying belief in the importance of education. In his introduction to the *Guide* Morey writes: "Though Nature Study is becoming popular, is being taught in most of the schools, and is encouraged in high places, many are still without the fold, failing to appreciate or understand the intense interest which those within feel in every living thing, in the stars above and the rocks below." The idea that certain species could become endangered didn't occur to Frank for nature seemed so prolific and there was nothing in the rules of the IWNHAS concerning conservation. Indeed some of his methods would be frowned upon today; the shooting and stuffing of birds and mammals for staged photographs, for instance, was common practice. Nevertheless, Frank was aware of the need for protection and in 1924, a year before his death, Frank bought the fifty acres of Borthwood Copse and gave it to the National Trust.

The wonders he found in nature as a boy continued to excite and delight Frank throughout his life. In his *Guide* he remarks on the "consistent beauty that prevails throughout Nature. When it does not appeal to the eye through the aesthetic sense it is usually apparent to the intellect from its fitness of design and adaption to environment." And though the beauty of a landscape or seascape may be easy to appreciate we can find beauty of form and design in a beetle or a fly, or a lowly flower.

Remarkable Islanders

⁂ PUBLIC HEALTH PIONEER ⁂

ARTHUR HILL HASSALL

While leaving the offices of the medical journal, the *Lancet*, one day Dr Arthur Hill Hassall felt "a loud ringing cough" come on quite suddenly. "I had experienced a similar fit of coughing a day or two earlier, and this time a little blood followed." It was fibroid phthisis of the right lung which confined him to his bed for long periods and the road back to health was a slow and weary one. He was taken to Hastings and spent some time at St Leonards before a final move to Ventnor for the winter was advised. The year of his illness was 1866 and Hassall was to spend the next ten years of his life on the island and leave a remarkable legacy in the shape of the Royal National Hospital for Consumption.

Arthur Hill Hassall, physician, surgeon and apothecary, was a medical pioneer who, according to his biographer, did more than any other single individual to improve the health of Britain's great cities and became a household name in the process. He used his microscope as a weapon to reveal the wholesale adulteration of food and drink – coffee had chicory and potato flour added, sugar was infested with mites, water tainted with lead, bread with alum. His published reports in the *Lancet*, which covered all the main articles of consumption, named the perpetrators and had an extraordinary impact. "A gun suddenly fired into a rookery could not cause greater commotion," wrote the *Quarterly Review*, and Edwin Chadwick used the reports in Parliament as ammunition to force public health issues to the front. This agitation lead directly to the anti-adulteration Food Bill of 1860.

Hassall's work on microscopic freshwater life lead him to investigate London's water supply which was polluted by cholera. His reports in the *Lancet* on the state of the Thames made scary reading and he gave invaluable evidence at a Parliamentary Committee of Enquiry into the metropolitan water supply.

If Chadwick, as Chairman of the General Board of Health was firing the gun, it was Hassall who supplied the bullets. His work was instrumental in procuring a new water supply for London.

In 1842, three years before the Great Famine followed the failure of the Irish potato crop, Hassall had revealed how fungi might destroy fruit and vegetables; his letters to the press on the causes of the failure were, however, largely ignored. A pioneer with the microscope, Hassall was also gifted with the pen. He was author of a *History of British Freshwater Algae*, acknowledged as a classic, and his *Microscopic Anatomy of the Human Body* was the first complete English language book on the subject.

All this work preceded his arrival on the island. He took up residence in Ventnor where the climate "is scarcely to be equalled in Great Britain." Ventnor was already renowned as a popular health resort luring the sickly resident of the crowded city, providing relief from the grime and smog of the burgeoning industrial towns – at least to those who could afford it. It struck Hassall that Ventnor and the Undercliff, with its sheltered, south-facing aspect, mild climate and clean sea air was the perfect site for a hospital or sanatorium for the benefit of those, like himself, who suffered from diseases of the lungs. The Brompton Hospital for Consumption, though invaluable, was in London's carbon-laden, impure atmosphere and hardly conducive to speedy recovery.

Hassal's dream of a hospital "for those for whom art can do least and nature most" could not be realised without money; he therefore drew up a prospectus to build eight blocks of semi-detached houses, each to accommodate six patients and each patient to have a separate bedroom facing south. Two sitting rooms in each house were to be shared by the six patients. The response was beyond Hassall's expectations and just two years after his arrival, in 1868, the first block was completed and opened for patients.

Once again Hassall was leading the way. His hospital was designed upon the 'Separate System' which kept patients separated as far as was practicable; this was well before the infectious nature of tuberculosis had been proved. Eleven blocks were completed in a terrace stretching for a quarter of a mile. With room for 240 patients and 60 staff, over 100,000 people received treatment during the 96 years the hospital was open. It was a national institution that attracted international attention and was much visited. The British Medical Association wrote in their journal, following a visit in 1881, "the Ventnor Hospital was much admired; no other hospital in Europe can compare with it for the completeness with which the Cottage system is carried out and for the combination of comfort and scientific fitness for its peculiar purpose."

Hassall lived at St Catherine's House in Church Street where he had "a commodious laboratory built where original investigations were carried out and analyses made." He paid for two assistants which left him struggling financially. On leaving Ventnor in 1877, Hassall was presented with a Service of Silver and a purse of three hundred guineas. When he died in San Remo, Italy, on 9 April 1894 he left his wife virtually penniless.

The photograph of Hassall, aged about 45, was carefully staged; behind him is the silver statuette awarded him for his services to public health; by his left hand is the Ross microscope with which "many vastly important facts were to be brought to light;" and nearby the well-received books he authored.

Remarkable Islanders

⚜ The Hurricane Pilot ⚜

Hurricane at Suez

Johnnie White was just nineteen when he joined the RAF after reading an advertisement in the paper: it read "Swap your overalls for a Flying Suit." It was towards the end of 1941 and Johnnie was in his second year at J.S. White's Somerton factory working on aircraft production. His job was a Reserved Occupation of national importance and he could only leave it if he trained as aircrew who were desperately needed to fly the aircraft coming out of the factories. By the end of the war Pilot Officer 'Chalkie' White had flown his maximum number of missions, earnt the Distinguished Flying Cross, and lead a bizarre sortie credited with the capture of twenty enemy troop-carrying ships.

Arthur John Bertram White was born on 31 March 1922 at Shanklin. His father was a decorator and undertaker, his grandfather a general builder who, in 1897, built the Jubilee Clocktower on Shanklin seafront. Johnnie left school at fourteen to become an apprentice mechanic but went to White's at the outbreak of war. After attending evening classes at Sandown in order to pass the required examinations he joined the RAF in December 1941 and was sent to Scarborough for three months of lectures. After a month at Perth on Tiger Moths he was assessed as 'pilot material' and sent to South Africa where his 'real' training began.

Under the Empire Air Training scheme Johnnie learnt to fly in Tiger Moths before switching to the more powerful and advanced Harvard trainer. While waiting at Durban for transport home at the completion of training in 1942, a draft of fifty recruits, Johnnie among them, was sent at the last minute to Egypt to fly Hurricanes. After journeying across the length of Africa by railway, lorry, flying boat and steamer he spent some time at Ismailiya, Suez learning to fly Hurricanes before his final posting to No. 6 Squadron in

Tunisia just as the campaign in North Africa came to an end.

In the spring of 1944 the Squadron re-located to Italy for operations along the Adriatic and Albanian coast. Coincidentally, the departing commanding officer of the squadron was another islander – "Tank Buster" Morrison-Bell from Bembridge. Italy was in the throes of bitter fighting, when Sgt AJB White, always known as 'Chalkie,' began flying sorties against the Germans. Strikes against coastal shipping, harbour installations and heavily defended coastal gun positions formed a large part of the squadron's operational flying though they tried to avoid unnecessary land targets to keep civilian casualties to the minimum. In December 1944 he was promoted 'from the ranks' and commissioned Pilot Officer.

In March 1945 P/O White led a section of aircraft equipped with rockets to attack an enemy strongpoint at Zegar in Yugoslavia. They encountered intense anti-aircraft fire causing damage to the aircraft, but a number of enemy transport vehicles were destroyed and strongpoints damaged. On many other missions P/O White carried out very effective reconnaissances of enemy held harbours on the Istrian peninsula by flying at great risk at a low level. Such missions were to earn him the Distinguished Flying Cross "for gallantry and devotion to duty in air operations."

Perhaps his most extraordinary mission occurred as the war in Europe was nearing its end. At the beginning of May 1945 four pilots took off from Prkos on the Yugoslav mainland (Johnnie says they were the only sober ones in the mess) with orders to make contact with enemy vessels from Trieste. It was believed they would try and surrender, the only sensible course now open to them. 'Chalkie' was to lead the sortie; they found sixteen enemy troopships in convoy and made a dummy attack, launching their rockets harmlessly into the sea. A white flag was hoisted and lowered again so a second attack was made to help them make up their minds. Soon they were all running up white flags and ships were emerging from harbours and inlets as resistance gave way to surrender. The sortie led by P/O John White was officially credited with the capture of twenty troopships on that extraordinary day!

It wasn't long after this incident that Chalkie White was posted back to Suez at the School of Gunnery and Bombing. Rumour has it that the RAF were trying to claim prize money for the captured ships and they wanted him out of the way, unavailable as a witness, but John himself doesn't believe this. Though the war was over he couldn't go home yet, but was posted to Palestine and flew a number of missions to intercept ships carrying illegal Jewish immigrants. He finally made it home in 1946 and, after a summer operating speedboats at Shanklin (during which time he attempted to rescue the occupants of a light aeroplane that crashed in Sandown Bay), returned to the job as mechanic he gave up when the war started, swapping his flying suit for his overalls once more.

PILOT OFFICER WHITE (2ND LEFT)

When asked if there had been any bad, sad or glad moments in his career as a Hurricane pilot, he recalls: "there was a mad moment when, on returning from a sortie, I discovered Befnal, one of my ground crew, had fixed an oil leak before I took off by wrapping his handkerchief round it, and that was all that kept me in the air. There was a sad moment when a pilot from another flight asked to fly with me because I seemed to attract all the action. On our next mission he was shot down and killed."

On his 80th birthday Johnnie White took to the air once more in a dual control Tiger Moth, the aircraft in which he trained, taking the controls again with ease. Some things you never forget.

Remarkable Islanders

⚜ Unpredictable Uffa ⚜

Uffa, 1933

Uffa Fox, yachtsman, designer, writer, adventurer, was loved or hated but seldom ignored. "His life was one long campaign for the freedom of the human spirit," wrote friend and sailing companion the Duke of Edinburgh. He was a man who aroused passions in others for there burned a fire within that couldn't be doused. A genuine eccentric whose brash self-confidence was twinned with a mercurial charm, there was, nevertheless, a darker side – his temper, sometimes erupting into violence, was as unstable as his finances and he could be selfish and irresponsible. His successful designs – from the Flying Fifteen dinghy to the airborne lifeboat – made him known the world over, and his association with royalty brought him fame and notoriety.

Uffa Fox was born on 15 January 1898 and spent most of his childhood at Cowes. From an early age he developed a deep love for the sea and when he left school it was for a seven year apprenticeship in boatbuilding and design at S.E. Saunders. This was interrupted by two years war service with the Royal Naval Air Service where his "free spirit" resulted in frequent clashes with authority. A more appreciative crowd he found in the Sea Scouts and at 21 he was appointed Scout Master. Illustrative of Uffa's cavalier attitude was the trip he planned in July 1921 to sail and row across the Channel and up the Seine to Paris in a whaleboat. He neglected to tell the parents of the boys he took, who were sworn to secrecy, and the Sea Scout committee, charged with irresponsibility by the outraged parents, resigned en bloc.

At 21 he set up his own boatbuilding business which gave him the freedom to disappear whenever the opportunity to crew on a boat across the Atlantic arose. He began designing National Fourteen Footers with the intention of producing a dinghy with a planing hull and with *Avenger* he succeeded beyond his wildest expectations. In the 1928 season she gained fifty-two firsts, two seconds and three thirds from fifty-seven starts. She became a legend, much copied, and order books for Uffa's designs swelled. Uffa found time to marry Alma Phillips in 1925 but when he turned up in dirty white plimsolls and looking like a "fugitive from the workhouse," she nearly called it off. Typical of Uffa, there was no honeymoon because he wanted to go sailing afterwards!

After *Avenger* sailors from all over the world sought him out. He next turned his attention to sailing canoes and with *Valiant* and *East Anglian*, designed by Uffa, he and Roger de Quincy lifted the New York Canoe Club's International Trophy, which had not left America since it was first raced for in 1866. Despite his success Uffa's finances were shaky and it was threats by his bank manager that forced Uffa to finally agree to write a book. *Sailing, Seamanship and Yacht Construction*, a blend of information, adventure and philosophy, was an immediate success. He went on to write many others, as well as articles for magazines and was a much sought after speaker.

Uffa's treatment of Alma was shabby; she was aware of his infidelity but his affair with Cherry, a boarding-house keeper from Bembridge, finally lead to her departure. She quietly divorced him and Uffa married Cherry in 1941. Cherry's son Bobbie joined the Air Sea Rescue branch of the RAF and his stories of the plight of aircrew lost at sea made a great impression. So Uffa had the idea for an Airborne Lifeboat which could be carried beneath aeroplanes and dropped by parachute to survivors of ditched aircraft. They had sails, engine, survival kit and instructions how to sail and Uffa's invention, which he thought of as his most fulfilling design, lead to the saving of the lives of many aircrew.

The war years were good for Uffa, full order books for his airborne lifeboats

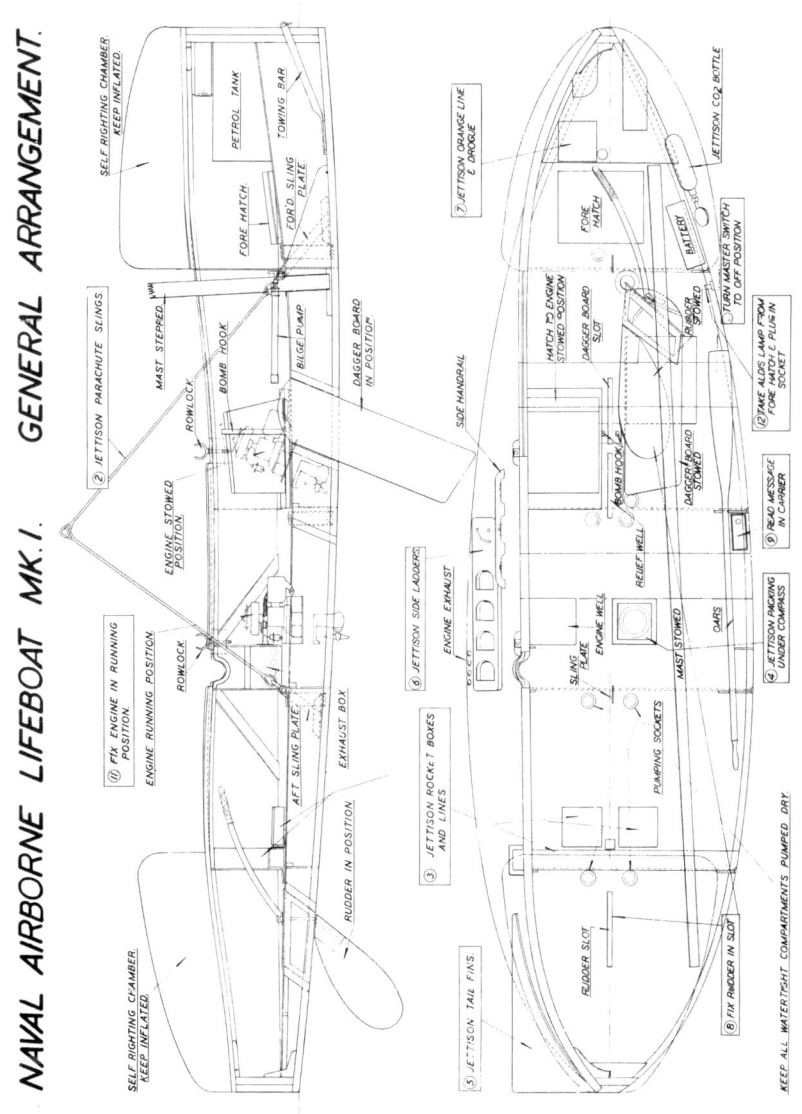

NAVAL AIRBORNE LIFEBOAT MkI

brought some stability to his finances. But the years of austerity after the war were equally lean and Uffa was approached by Fairey Aviation and asked to design moulded boats for their new marine division. Out of this association came the Firefly, a twelve foot One Design, which was selected for the 1948 Olympics and Uffa went on to design an impressive list of popular boats.

Uffa's most successful post-war design, the Flying Fifteen, was a planing keelboat the main lines of which were sketched while lounging in the bath. Out of that design came a range of planing keelboats from the Flying Ten to the Flying Twenty Five and a series of cruiser/racer yachts from the Flying Twenty Five through to the Flying Fifty. Uffa became great friends with Prince Philip the Duke of Edinburgh and they sailed together many times in the Flying Fifteen, *Coweslip*, which is on display at the Classic Boat Museum, Newport. His association with Prince Philip made him something of a celebrity; he was a regular visitor to Buckingham Palace and a frequent guest aboard the Royal Yacht. Uffa wasn't so successful in his private life; his philandering lead to Cherry's departure in 1948 amid much acrimony. Then in 1956 he married a French lady, Yvonne Bernard, though Uffa spoke no French and Yvonne no English!

Uffa's career became more and more bizarre. He could play the piano and belt out a sea shanty and recorded an LP, 'Uffa Sings.' He appeared on TV and radio shows and even compered a concert. He continued to design boats until his death in 1972. The Duke of Edinburgh said of him:- "There is a tendency nowadays to imagine that everything new must be scientific or rational. Uffa Fox as a helmsman in his day was a world beater, and as a designer of boats he is also a world beater. I can state categorically that there is practically nothing scientific or rational about Mr Fox. Like all great designers his genius is entirely human."

Remarkable Islanders

THE SWASHBUCKLING CAPTAIN

SIR EDWARD HORSEY

Adventurer, sea rover and Channel privateer, Throckmorton plotter against Catholic Queen Mary, loyal and dutiful servant of Protestant Queen Elizabeth, knight, Captain of the Wight and friend of pirates, Privy Councillor, able naval and military commander, diplomatist and ultimately victim of the plague. Edward Horsey was all these; his epitaph in St Thomas' Church, Newport, inscribed upon his monument, a recumbent knight in armour, reads: "And as he lived holily so he executed holily his particular duties."

England's turmoil during the religious struggle known as the Reformation presented opportunities for the daring and adventurous to make their name and perhaps their fortune. England was in the midst of a tussle between Protestantism and Catholicism; under Queen Mary, who ascended the throne in 1553, the pendulum swung back towards Rome. Her marriage to Philip of Spain, soon to be crowned Philip II, was deeply unpopular with the country and there was a general belief that not only was she striving to make England Catholic, but was subordinating English interests to those of the Spanish state.

The French, keen to prevent Philip of Spain from reaching England, flooded the Channel with as many ships as they could equip and man. Disaffected young men from honourable families, indignant at Mary's persecutions, slipped over the Channel and joined them. The French supplied them with ships, arms and money; these young adventurers sailing in their heavily armed privateers, plundered Flemish and Spanish ships and swore they would not let Philip set foot on English shores.

Among this band of piratical opportunists was Edward Horsey, born of a good Dorsetshire family. Also mixed up with these headstrong young men was Sir Henry Dudley who, with Francis Throckmorton, hatched a plot to depose Mary in favour of her half-sister Elizabeth. The conspirators, mostly minor members of the gentry and peerage and a few royal servants, met in a London house of entertainment called Arundel's. Here 'Ned' Horsey spoke of his preparations on the Isle of Wight where he had arranged for Uvedale, Captain of Yarmouth Castle, to ensure a safe harbour for the invasion of exiles and mercenaries who were to secure the island then march on London. Money to hire ships and mercenaries was to come from the Exchequer where Dudley had contacts; £50,000 was to be stolen and smuggled abroad to France where the plotters had friends amongst the Protestant exiles.

French support was essential and Dudley and Horsey went to France and were given an audience with Henry II. The French King, who had just signed a 5-year truce with Spain, gave them some money but only vague promises of support. Wotton, the English ambassador to France, got wind of the plot and informed Queen Mary. The plot collapsed and Uvedale on the Isle of Wight and twenty others were seized and committed to the tower. Edward Horsey and Sir Henry Dudley escaped to France and were received openly at Court. Horsey and his comrades were proclaimed traitors and the Queen instructed Noailles, the French ambassador, to deliver up "those wretches, those heretics, those traitorous, execrable villains" to her charge. Uvedale and seven others were convicted and executed. Henry II of France, while promising to apprehend the traitors, instead furnished them with ships. Horsey and other refugees from Mary began plundering Spanish ships again; before the summer was out they had taken "divers good prizes" and "did that they should take more."

On the death of Mary, Elizabeth was crowned Queen and Horsey and the other exiles were no longer outlaws. Lord Robert Dudley intervened on Horsey's behalf; but even without Dudley's help Edward Horsey, who had risked the rope and gallows by his plunder of the Spanish galleons, could fairly claim some reward from the new regime. He received his reward belatedly when he was made a knight on his appointment, in 1565, to the Captaincy of the Isle of Wight following the death of Sir Richard Worsley.

Of his years as Captain of the island from 1565 to his death in 1582 we know little for certain. He garrisoned the forts built by his predecessors and imported saltpetre so he could make his own gunpowder. During Elizabeth's reign the Channel was rife with corsairs and pirates, many of them English, some of them islanders. Mead Hole, between East Cowes and Wootton Creek was a notorious pirate anchorage, and Horsey was instructed to make a count of the shipping there and take necessary measures to help rid the English Channel of such buccaneers.

Being an old sea dog himself Horsey had some sympathy with them and even admitted receiving "presents of spices, sweetmeats, and canary wine;" he wasn't averse to using the pirates to his advantage either as when he instructed John Vaughan to act as scout looking out for signs of the expected Spanish fleet. But Sir Edward did not condone piracy and privateering and at times came down hard on them. Captain Edward Denny had his two prize ships impounded and Horsey had the famous *Castle of Comfort*, which had a history of piracy, laid up. If, as they say, it takes a thief to catch a thief, then Sir Edward Horsey was well qualified to help stamp out piracy.

In 1567 a rebellion broke out in the North lead by Thomas Percy, Earl of Northumberland, and Charles Neville, Earl of Westmorland. They advanced south into Yorkshire but it petered out when it met royal forces under the Earl of Sussex. Sir Edward was in command of Clinton's cavalry on the Tyne; he had nothing but contempt for the plotters and their cowardice and the insurgents were ruthlessly hunted down and strung up by the wayside. Sir Edward's skill as a diplomatist was tested when, in 1573, he assisted in the peace negotiations between the Huguenots and the French King. He was also appointed ambassador to the Netherlands.

As Captain of the Wight, Horsey was expected to make Carisbrooke Castle his home and base. But Horsey, whose French wife obstinately remained in France, shocked island gentry by preferring to live with a lively young widow, Dowsabelle Mills of Haseley Manor, and kept an open house. In common with other governors of the island, Horsey enjoyed hunting. A day's hare-coursing or hawking was followed by a generous feast and entertainment at Haseley. It was in the arms of Dowsabelle that Sir Edward succumbed to the plague, in 1582.

If Sir Edward Horsey, the jovial sea-dog, made no great impact on island affairs, neither did he leave any dark deeds as legacy. He was even-handed in his administration of affairs and was generally popular with island inhabitants. He was no "unlettered seaman" but a well-educated gentleman. He was accused of consorting with pirates who found sanctuary during his captaincy in that part of town known as Castlehold. Yet he indignantly denied this accusation. Sir Edward was staunchly protestant but with the easy social morals characteristic of his day. But there is one deed for which he will always be credited. Before Sir Edward's captaincy the island had "not one hare;" to remedy this Horsey offered a lamb for every hare introduced. So successful was this ploy that the island now has a thriving population of hares!

Further Reading

Galloper Jack,
BROUGH SCOTT, MACMILLAN, 2003.

Adventure,
J.E.B. SEELY, WILLIAM HEINEMAN, LONDON, 1930.

The Isle of Wight Rifles,
D.J. QUIGLEY.

Smugglers of the Isle of Wight,
RICHARD J. HUCHINGS, IW COUNTY PRESS, 1984 ED.

The Lifeboats of Brighstone Bay,
CHRISTOPHER J. WILLIS & EDWARD H. ROBERTS, IW COUNTY PRESS, 1985 ED.

Rugged but Golden,
JOHN MATTHEWS

Letters Archaeological and Historical,
REV E. BOUCHER JAMES, VOLS I & II, HENRY FROWDE, 1896.

Captain of the Wight,
FRANK COWPER, SEELEY & CO, LONDON, 1889.

Sea Battles,
MICHAEL SANDERSON, DAVID & CHARLES, 1975.

Lords, Captains and Governors of the IW,
R.K. SHERIDON, HMSO, 1974.

The Scandal of Sophie Dawes,
MARJORIE BOWEN, JOHN LANE, 1935

The Man Who Knew Too Much,
STEPHEN INWOOD, MACMILLAN, 2002.

Lecture,
BY ALLAN CHAPMAN RECORDED IN THE PROCEEDINGS OF THE
ROYAL INSTITUTION OF GREAT BRITAIN, 67, PP 239-275, 1996.

The Story of the Royal National Hospital,
VENTNOR, E.F. LAIDLAW, 1990. BY CANDLELIGHT.

Guide to the Natural History of the Isle of Wight,
ED. FRANK MOREY, IW COUNTY PRESS, 1909.

Uffa Fox: A Personal Biography,
JUNE DIXON, ANGUS & ROBERTSON, 1978.

Acknowledgements

For the reproduction of illustrations and photographs I would like to acknowledge the following organisations and people:-

Photo, Edward Horsey's tomb, the Vicar and Churchwardens of Newport. Picture of Battle of Vigo Bay, from an oil painting by Ludolf Bakhuizen. Picture of Elizabeth Woodville, courtesy the Masters and Fellows of Queen's College, Cambridge. Engraving of Earl Rivers and Edward IV courtesy of Hulton Picture Library. Photo, James Buckett courtesy R.H. Buckett. Sophie Dawes, from a miniature by an unknown artist in the Musée Condé, Chantilly. Duc de Bourbon from a portrait by Pierre Denloux in the Musée Condé, Chantilly. Hooke's telescope courtesy of the Science Museum, London. Photo, William Russell's cottage, Brighstone, R.H. Shotter. Photo, Edgar Greenshield, reproduced from the book by John Matthews. John Sibbick for permission to reproduce his artists impression of 'Polacanthus Foxii'. Robin McInnes for permission to reproduce the chromolithograph entitled "Lifeboat rescue on the back of the Wight."

I would like to thank Sheila Caws and the Local Reference Collection of the IWCC's Library Service; John Bloodworth for allowing me access to his private collection; my wife Jill for reading drafts and suggesting changes; and Coach House Publications for useful suggestions.